The Walam Olum

By

Daniel Garrison Brinton

Published by Left of Brain Books

Copyright © 2023 Left of Brain Books

ISBN 978-1-397-66708-3

First Edition

All rights reserved. No part of this publication may be reproduced, distributed, or transmitted in any form or by any means, including photocopying, recording, or other electronic or mechanical methods, without the prior written permission of the publisher, except in the case of brief quotations permitted by copyright law. Left of Brain Books is a division of Left Of Brain Onboarding Pty Ltd.

PUBLISHER'S PREFACE

About the Book

"This controversial work is purportedly a translation of a sequence of pictographs which give the epic of the Delawares, a tribe which lived in the central Eastern seaboard. Taken at face value, this would be one of the few actual written texts from Native North America, including a clear account of an eastward migration over the 'stone-hard water'. The source of the document, as well as aspects of the Delaware text, and some of the historical episodes have been called into question. I'm not going to rehash this discussion here, but offer some comments based on the content of the text.

Most likely, the Walam Olum was forged in the 19th Century by someone who was attempting to provide a mythological underpinning for the theory that Native Americans migrated from Asia at some point in the recent past. It is now believed that this migration took place between ten and fifteen thousand years ago. Instead of a mass emigration over a frozen ocean, it was a gradual infiltration by small groups. They weren't out to discover a new world, but simply following their food sources. Initially they moved over a land bridge that connected Asia and America (Behringia), which was exposed at the time by the the greatly lowered Ice Age sea levels. When the glaciers contracted at the end of the Ice Age, the conventional theory is that a 'corridor' through western Canada was created, which served as a migration route south into North America. Another theory is that people could have taken a sea route along the Canadian coast to bypass the ice sheets. In any case, the archeological record indicates that it took hundreds or thousands of years for people to get from Siberia to the shores of the Atlantic."

(Quote from sacred-texts.com)

About the Author

Daniel Garrison Brinton (1837 - 1899)

"Daniel Garrison Brinton (May 13, 1837-July 31, 1899), was an American archaeologist and ethnologist.

He was born in Thornbury, Pennsylvania. After graduating from Yale University in 1858, Brinton studied at Jefferson Medical College for two years and spent the next travelling in Europe. He continued his studies at Paris and Heidelberg. From 1862 to 1865, during the American Civil War, he was a surgeon in the Union army, acting during 1864-1865 as surgeon-in-charge of the U.S. Army general hospital at Quincy, Illinois.

After the war, Brinton practiced medicine in West Chester, Pennsylvania for several years; was the editor of a weekly periodical, the Medical and Surgical Reporter, in Philadelphia from 1874 to 1887; became professor of ethnology and archaeology in the Academy of Natural Sciences in Philadelphia in 1884; and was professor of American linguistics and archaeology in the University of Pennsylvania from 1886 until his death.

He was a member of numerous learned societies in the United States and in Europe and was president at different times of the Numismatic and Antiquarian Society of Philadelphia, of the American Folk-Lore Society and of the American Association for the Advancement of Science.

Brinton, at his presidential address in August 1895, advocated theories of scientific racism that were pervasive at the time. As Charles Lofgren notes in his book, The Plesy Case, Brinton "accepted the 'psychical unity' throughout the human species," he noted that "all races were 'not equally endowed,' which disqualified them from the atmosphere of modern enlightenment.""

(Quote from wikipedia.org)

CONTENTS

PUBLISHER'S PREFACE
- PART I. 1
- PART II. 9
- PART III. 15
- PART IVa. 23
- PART IVb. 29
- PART IVc. 36
- PART Va. 44
- PART Vb. 50
- PART Vc. 56

PART I.

1. At first, in that place, at all times, above the earth,

1. Sayewi talli wemiguma wokgetaki,

2. On the earth, [was] an extended fog, and there the great Manito was.

2. Hackung kwelik owanaku wak yutali Kitanitowit-essop.

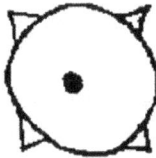

3. At first, forever, lost in space, everywhere, the great Manito was.

3. Sayewis hallemiwis nolemiwi elemamik Kitanitowit-essop.

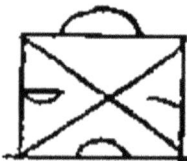

4. He made the extended land and the sky.

4. Sohawalawak kwelik hakik owak [read, woak] awasagamak.

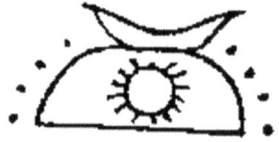

5. He made the sun, the moon, the stars.

5. Sohalawak gishuk nipahum alankwak.

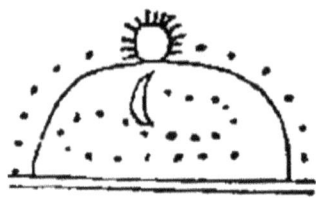

6. He made them all to move evenly.

6. Wemi-sohalawak yulikyuchaan.

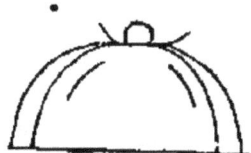

7. Then the wind blew violently, and it cleared, and the water flowed off far and strong.

7. Wich-owagan kshakan moshakwat [Var. moshakguat.] kwelik kshipehelep.

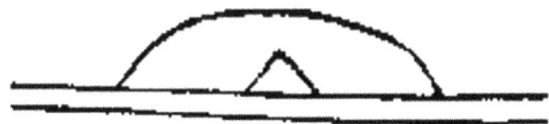

8. And groups of islands grew newly, and there remained.

8. Opeleken mani-menak delsin-epit.

9. Anew spoke the great Manito, a manito to manitos,

9. Lappinup Kitanitowit manito manitoak.

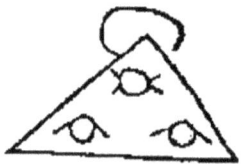

10. To beings, mortals, souls and all,

10. Owiniwak angelatawiwak chichankwak wemiwak.

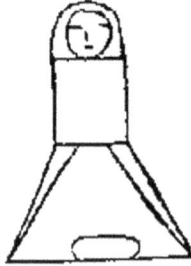

11. And ever after he was a manito to men, and their grandfather.

11. Wtenk manito jinwis lennowak mukom.

12. He gave the first mother, the mother of beings.

12. Milap netami gaho owini gaho.

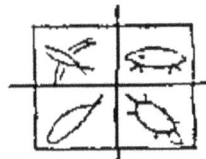

13. He gave the fish, he gave the turtles, he gave the beasts, he gave the birds.

13. Namesik milap, tulpewik milap, awesik milap, cholensak milap.

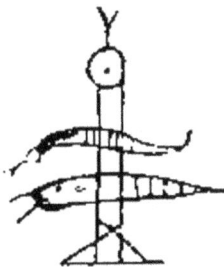

14. But an evil Manito made evil beings only, monsters,

14. Makimani shak sohalawak makowini nakowak amangamek.

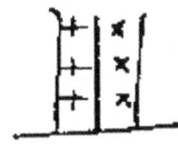

15. He made the flies, he made the gnats.

15. Sohalawak uchewak, sohalawak pungusak.

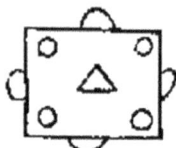

16. All beings were then friendly.

16. Nitisak wemi owini w'delisinewuap.

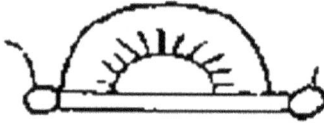

17. Truly the manitos were active and kindly

17. Kiwis, wunand wishimanitoak essopak.

18. To those very first men, and to those first mothers; fetched them wives,

18. Nijini netami lennowak, nigoha netami okwewi, nantine'wak.

19. And fetched them food, when first they desired it.

19. Gattamin netami mitzi nijini nantine'.

20. All had cheerful knowledge, all had leisure, all thought in gladness.

20. Wemi wingi-namenep, wemi ksinelendamep, wemi wullatemanuwi.

21. But very secretly an evil being, a mighty magician, came on earth,

21. Shukand eli-kimi mekenikink wakon powako init'ako.

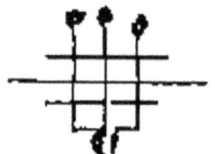

22. And with him brought badness, quarreling, unhappiness,

22. Mattalogas pallalogas maktaton owagan payat-chik yutali.

23. Brought bad weather, brought sickness, brought death.

23. Maktapan payat, wihillan payat, mboagan payat.

24. All this took place of old on the earth, beyond the great tide-water, at the first.

24. Won wemi wiwunch kamik atak kitahikan netamaki epit.

PART II.

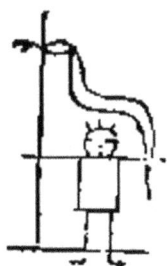

1. Long ago there was a mighty snake and beings evil to men.

1. Wtilamo maskanako anup lennowak makowini essopak.

2. This mighty snake hated those who were there (and) greatly disquieted those whom he hated.

2. Maskanako shingalusit nijini essopak shawelendamep eken shingalan.

3. They both did harm, they both injured each other, both were not in peace.

3. Nisliawi` palliton, nishawi machiton, nishawi matta lungtindowin.

4. Driven from their homes they fought with this murderer.

4. Mattapewi wiki nihanlowit mekwazoan.

5. The mighty snake firmly resolved to harm the men.

5. Maskanako gishi penatiwelendamep lennowak owini palliton.

6. He brought three persons, he brought a monster, he brought a rushing water.

6. Nakowa petonep, amangam petonep, akopehella petonep.

7. Between the hills the water rushed and rushed, dashing through and through, destroying much.

7. Pehella pehella, pohoka pohoka, eshohok eshohok, palliton palliton.

8. Nanabush, the Strong White One, grandfather of beings, grandfather of men, was on the Turtle Island.

8. Tulapit menapit Nanabotish maskaboush owinimokom linowimokom.

9. There he was walking and creating, as he passed by and created the turtle.

9. Gishikin-pommixin tulagishattenlohxin.

10. Beings and men all go forth, they walk in the floods and shallow waters, down stream thither to the Turtle Island.

10. Owini linowi wemoltin, Pehella gahani pommixin, Nahiwi tatalli tulapin.

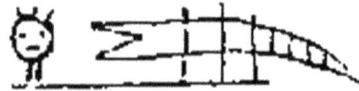

11. There were many monster fishes, which ate some of them.

11. Amanganek makdopannek alendyuwek metzipannek.

12. The Manito daughter, coming, helped with her canoe, helped all, as they came and came.

12. Manito-dasin mokol-wichemap, Palpal payat payat wemichemap.

13. [And also] Nanabush, Nanabush, the grandfather of all, the grandfather of beings, the grandfather of men, the grandfather of the turtle.

13. Nanaboush Nanaboush wemimokom, Wimimokom linnimokom tulamokom.

14. The men then were together on the turtle, like to turtles.

14. Linapi-ma tulapi-ma tulapewi tapitawi.

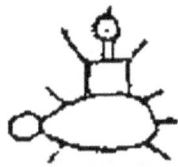

15. Frightened on the turtle, they prayed on the turtle that what was spoiled should be restored.

14

15. Wishanem tulpewi pataman tulpewi poniton wuliton.

16. The water ran off, the earth dried, the lakes were at rest, all was silent, and the mighty snake departed.

16. Kshipehelen penkwihilen, Kwamipokho sitwalikho, Maskan wagan palliwi palliwi.

PART III.

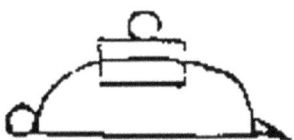

1. After the rushing waters (had subsided) the Lenape of the turtle were close together, in hollow houses, living together there.

1. Pehella wtenk lennapeva tulapewini psakwiken woliwikgun wittank talli.

2. It freezes where they abode, it snows where they abode, it storms where they abode, it is cold where they abode.

2. Topan-akpinep, wineu-akpinep, kshakan-akpinep, thupin akpinep.

3. At this northern place they speak favorably of mild, cool (lands), with many deer and buffaloes.

3. Lowankwaminkwulaton wtakan tihill kelik meshautang sili ewak.

4. As they journeyed, some being strong, some rich, they separated into house-builders and hunters;

4. Chintanes-sin powalessin peyachik wikhichik pokwihil.

5. The strongest, the most united, the purest, were the hunters.

5. Eluwi-chitanesit eluwi takauwesit, elowi chiksit, elowichik delsinewo.

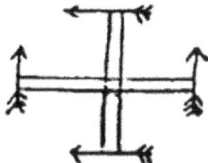

6. The hunters showed themselves at the north, at the east, at the south, at the west.

6. Lowaniwi, wapaniwi, shawaniwi, wunkeniwi, elowichik apakachik.

7. In that ancient country, in that northern country, in that turtle country, the best of the Lenape were the Turtle men.

7. Lumowaki, lowanaki tulpenaki elowaki tulapiwi linapiwi.

8. All the cabin fires of that land were disquieted, and all said to their priest, "Let us go."

8. Wemiako yagawan tendki lakkawelendam nakopowa wemi owenluen atam.

9. To the Snake land to the east they went forth, going away, earnestly grieving.

9. Akhokink wapaneu wemoltin palliaal kitelendam aptelendam.

10. Split asunder, weak, trembling, their land burned, they went, torn and broken, to the Snake Island.

10. Pechimuin shakowen [Var. showoken] nungihillan lusasaki pikihil pokwihil akomenaki.

11. Those from the north being free, without care, went forth from the land of snow, in different directions.

11. Nihillapewin komelendam lowaniwi wemiten chihillen maniaken.

12. The fathers of the Bald Eagle and the White Wolf remain along the sea, rich in fish and muscles.

12. Namesuagipek pokhapockhapek guneunga waplanewa ouken waptumewi ouken.

13. Floating up the streams in their canoes, our fathers were rich, they were in the light, when they were at those islands.

13. Amokolon nallahemen agunouken pawasinep wapasinep akomenep.[Var. menakinep.]

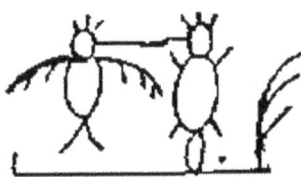

14. Head Beaver and Big Bird said, "Let us go to Snake Island," they said.

14. Wihlamok kicholen luchundi, Wematam akomen luchundi.

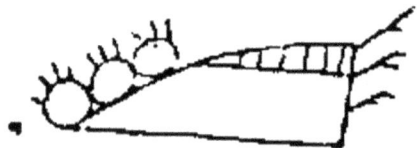

15. All say they will go along to destroy all the land.

15. Witehen wemiluen wemaken nihillen.

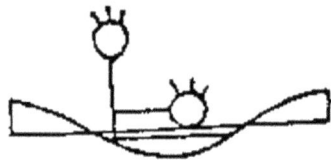

16. Those of the north agreed, Those of the east agreed. Over the water, the frozen sea, They went to enjoy it.

16. Nguttichin lowaniwi, Nguttichin wapaniwi, Agamunk topanpek Wulliton epannek.

17. On the wonderful slippery water, On the stone-hard water all went, On the great Tidal Sea, the muscle-bearing sea. They walk and walk, all of them.

17. Wulelemil w'shakuppek, Wemopannek hakhsinipek, Kitahikan pokhakhopek.

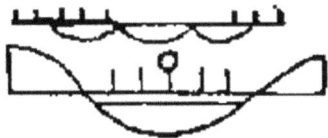

18. Ten thousand at night, All in one night, To the Snake Island, to the east, at night, They walk and walk, all of them.

18. Tellenchen kittapakki nillawi, Wemoltin gutikuni nillawi, Akomen wapanawaki nillawi, Ponskan, ponskan, wemiwi olini.

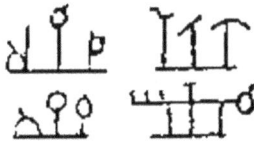

19. The men from the north, the east, the south, The Eagle clan, the Beaver clan, the Wolf clan, The best men, the rich men, the head men, Those with wives, those with daughters, those with dogs,

19. Lowanapi, wapanapi, shawanapi, Lanewapi, tamakwapi, tumewapi, Elowapi, powatapi, wilawapi, Okwisapi, danisapi, allumapil,

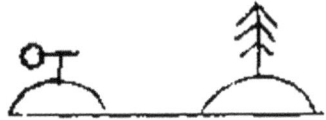

20. They all come, they tarry at the land of the spruce pines; Those from the west come with hesitation, Esteeming highly their old home at the Turtle land.

20. Wemipayat gune'unga shinaking, Wunkenapi chanelendam payaking, Allowelendam kowiyey tulpaking.

PART IVa.

1. Long ago the fathers of the Lenape were at the land of spruce pines.

1. Wulamo linapioken manup shinaking.

2. Hitherto the Bald Eagle band had been the pipe bearer,

2. Wapallanewa sittamaganat yukepechi wemima,

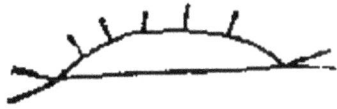

3. While they were searching for the Snake Island, that great and fine land.

3. Akhomenis michihaki wellaki kundokanup.

4. They having died, the hunters, about to depart, met together.

4. Angomelchik elowichik elmusichik menalting.

5. All say to Beautiful Head, "Be thou chief."

5. Wemilo kolawil sakima lissilma.

6. "Coming to the Snakes, slaughter at that Snake hill, that they leave it."

6. Akhopayat kihillalend akhopokho aski'waal.

7. All of the Snake tribe were weak, and hid themselves in the Swampy Vales.

7. Showihilla akhowemi gandhaton mashkipokhing.

8. After Beautiful Head, White Owl was chief at Spruce Pine land.

8. Wtenkolawil shinaking sakimanep wapagokhos.

9. After him, Keeping-Guard was chief of that people.

9. Wtenk nekama sakimanep janoto enolowin.

10. After him, Snow Bird was chief; he spoke of the south,

10. Wtenk nekama sakimanep chilili shawaniluen.

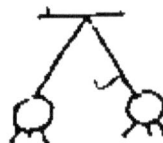

11. That our fathers should possess it by scattering abroad.

11. Wokenapi nitaton wullaton apakchikton.

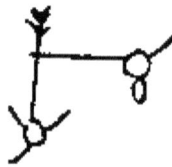

12. Snow Bird went south, White Beaver went east.

12. Shawaniwaen chilili, wapaniwaen tamakwi.

13. The Snake land was at the south, the great Spruce Pine land was toward the shore;

13. Akolaki shawanaki, kitshinaki shabiyaki.

14. To the east was the Fish land, toward the lakes was the buffalo land.

14. Wapanaki namesaki, pemapaki sisilaki.

15. After Snow Bird, the Seizer was chief, and all were killed,

15. Wtenk chilili sakimanep ayamek weminilluk.

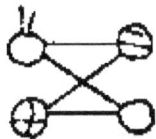

16. The robbers, the snakes, the evil men, the stone men.

16. Chikonapi akhonapi makatapi assinapi.

17. After the Seizer there were ten chiefs, and there was much warfare south and east.

17. Wtenk ayamek tellen sakimak machi tonanup shawapama.

18. After them, the Peaceable was chief at Snake land.

18. Wtenk nellamawa sakimanep langundowi akolaking.

19. After him, Not-Black was chief, who was a straight man.

19. Wtenk nekama sakimanep tasukamend shakagapipi.

PART IVb.

20. After him, Much-Loved was chief, a good man.

20. Wtenk nekama sakimanep pemaholend wulitowin.

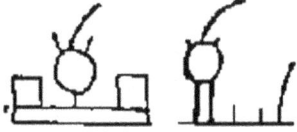

21. After him, No-Blood was chief, who walked in cleanliness.

21. Sagimawtenk matemik, sagimawtenk pilsohalin.

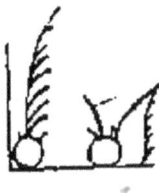

22. After him, Snow-Father was chief, he of the big teeth.

22. Sagimawtenk gunokeni, sagimawtenk mangipitak.

23. After him, Tally-Maker was chief, who made records.

23. Sagimawtenk olumapi, leksahowen sohalawak.

24. After him, Shiverer-with-Cold was chief, who went south to the corn land.

24. Sagimawtenk taguachi shawaniwaen minihaking.

25. After him, Corn-Breaker was chief, who brought about the planting of corn.

25. Sakimawtenk huminiend minigeman sohalgol.

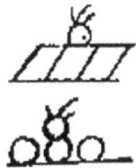

26. After him, the Strong-Man was chief, who was useful to the chieftains.

26. Sakinawtenk alkosohit sakimachik apendawi.

27. After him, the Salt-Man was chief, after him the Little-One was chief

27. Sawkimawtenk shiwapi, sakimatenk penkwoni.

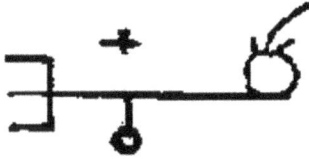

28. There was no rain, and no corn, so they moved further seaward.

28. Attasokelan attaminin wapaniwaen italissipek.

29. At the place of caves, in the buffalo land, they at last had food, on pleasant plain.

29. Oligonunk sisilaking nallimetzin kolakwaming.

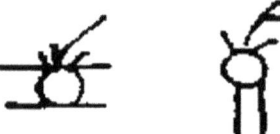

30. After the Little-One (came) the Fatigued; after him, the Stiff-One.

30. Wtenk penkwonwi wekwochella, wtenk nekama chingalsuwi.

31. After him, the Reprover; disliking him, and unwilling (to remain),

31. Wtenk nekama kwitikwond, slangelendam attagatta,

32. Being angry, some went off secretly, moving east.

32. Wundanuksin wapanickam [Var. wapanahan.] allendyachick kimimikwi.

33. The wise ones who remained made the Loving-One chief.

33. Gunehunga wetatamova wakaholend sakimalanop.

34. They settled again on the Yellow river, and had much corn on stoneless soil.

34. Wisawana lappi wittank michi mini madawasim.

35. All being friendly, the Affable was chief, the first of that name.

35. Weminitis tamenend sakimanep nekohatami.

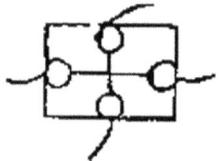

36. He was very good, this Affable, and came as a friend to all the Lenape.

36. Eluwiwulit matemenend wemi linapi nitis payat.

37. After this good one, Strong-Buffalo was chief and pipe-bearer.

37. Wtenk wulitma maskansisil sakimanep w'tamaganat.

38. Big-Owl was chief; White-Bird was chief.

38. Machigokloos sakimanep, wapkicholen sakimanep.

39. The Willing-One was chief and priest; he made festivals.

39. Wingenund sakimanep powatanep gentikalanep.

PART IVc.

40. Rich-Again was chief; the Painted-One was chief.

40. Lapawin sakimanep, wallama sakimanep.

41. White-Fowl was chief; again there was war, north and south.

41. Waptipatit sakimanep, lappi mahuk lowashawa.

42. The Wolf-wise-in Counsel was chief.

42. Wewoattan menatting tumaokan sakimanep.

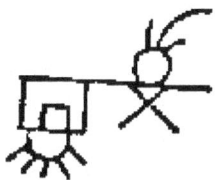

43. He knew how to make war on all; he slew Strong-Stone.

43. Nitatonep wemi palliton maskansini nihillanep.

44. The Always-Ready-One was chief; he fought against the Snakes.

44. Messissuwi sakimanep akowini pallitonep.

45. The Strong-Good-One was chief, he fought against the northerners.

45. Chitanwulit sakimanep lowanuski pallitonep.

46. The Lean-One was chief; he fought against the Tawa people.

46. Alokuwi sakimanep towakon pallitonep.

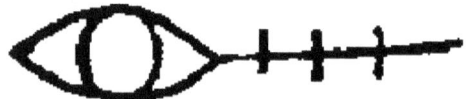

47. The Opossum-Like was chief; he fought in sadness,

47. Opekasit sakimanep sakhelendam pallitonepit.

48. And said, "They are many; let us go together to the east, to the sunrise."

48. Wapagishik yuknohokluen makeluhuk wapaneken.

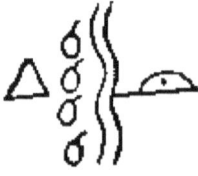

49. They separated at Fish river; the lazy ones remained there.

49. Tsebepieken nemassipi [Var. mixtisipi.] nolandowak gunehunga.

50. Cabin-Man was chief; the Talligewi possessed the east.

50. Yagawanend sakimanep talligewi wapawullaton.

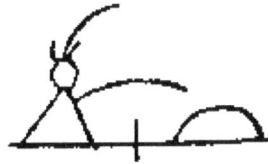

51. Strong-Friend was chief; he desired the eastern land.

51. Chitanitis sakimanep wapawaki gotatamen.

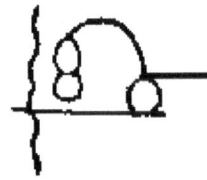

52. Some passed on east; the Talega ruler killed some of them.

52. Wapallendi pomisinep talegawil allendhilla.

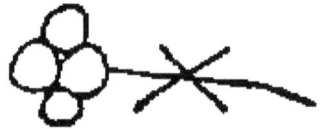

53. All say, in unison, "War, war."

53. Mayoksuwi wemilowi palliton palliton.

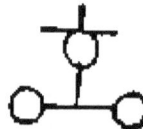

54. The Talamatan, friends from the north, come, and all go together.

54. Talamatan nitilowan payatchik wemiten.

55. The Sharp-One was chief, he was the pipe-bearer beyond the river.

55. Kinehepend sakimanep tamaganat sipakgamen.

56. They rejoiced greatly that they should fight and slay the Talega towns.

56. Wulatonwi makelima pallihilla talegawik.

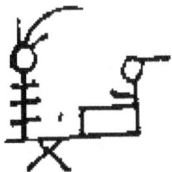

57. The Stirrer was chief; the Talega towns were too strong.

57. Pimokhasuwi sakimanep wsamimaskan talegawik.

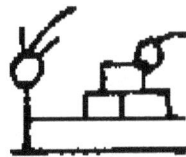

58. The Fire-Builder was chief; they all gave to him many towns.

58. Tenchekentit sakimanep wemilat makelinik.

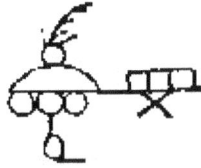

59. The Breaker-in-Pieces was chief, all the Talega go south.

59. Pagan chichilla sakimanep shawanewak wemi talega.

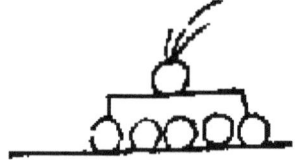

60. He-has-Pleasure was chief; all the people rejoice.

60. Hattan wulaton sakimanep, wingelendam wemi lennowak.

61. They stay south of the lakes; the Talamatan friends north of the lakes.

61. Shawanipekis gunehungind lowanipekis talamatanitis.

62. When Long-and-Mild was chief, those who were not his friends conspired.

62. Attabchinitis gishelendam gunitakan sakimanep.

63. Truthful-Man was chief, the Talamatans made war.

63. Linniwulamen sakimanep pallitonep talamatan.

64. Just-and-True was chief; the Talamatans trembled.

64. Shakagapewi sakimanep nungiwi talamatan.

PART Va.

1. All were peaceful, long ago, there at the Talega land.

1. Wemilangundo wulamo talli talegaking.

2. The Pipe-Bearer was chief at the White river.

2. Tamaganend sakimanep wapalaneng.

3. White-Lynx was chief, much corn was planted.

3. Wapushuwi sakimanep kelitgeman.

4. Good-and-Strong was chief; the people were many.

4. Wulitshinik sakimanep makdopannik.

5. The Recorder was chief; he painted the records.

5. Lekhihitin sakimanep wallamolumin.

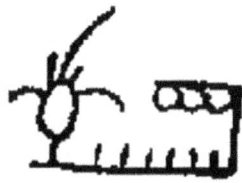

6. Pretty-Blue-Bird was chief; there was much fruit.

6. Kolachuisen sakimanep makeliming.

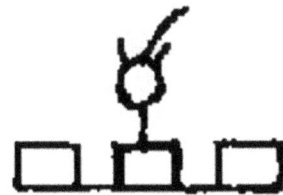

7. Always-There was chief; the towns were many.

7. Pematalli sakimanep makelinik.

8. Paddler-up-Stream was chief; he was much on the rivers,

8. Pepomahenem sakimanep makelaning.

9. Little-Cloud was chief; many departed,

9. Tankawon sakimanep makeleyachik,

10. The Nanticokes and the Shawnees going to the south.

10. Nentegowi shawanowi shawanaking.

11. Big-Beaver was chief, at the White Salt Lick.

11. Kichitamak sakimanep wapahoning.

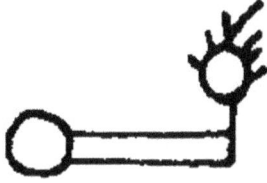

12. The Seer, the praised one, went to the west.

12. Onowutok awolagan wunkenahep.

13. He went to the west, to the southwest, to the western villages.

13. Wtinpakitonis wunshawononis wunkiwikwotank.

14. The Rich-Down-River-Man was chief, at Talega river.

14. Pawanami sakimanep taleganah.

15. The Walker was chief; there was much war.

15. Lokwelend sakimanep makpalliton.

16. Again with the Tawa people, again with the Stone people, again with the northern people.

16. Lappi towako lappi sinako lappi lowako.

17. Grandfather-of-Boats was chief; he went to lands in boats.

17. Mokolmokom sakimanep mokolakolin.

18. Snow-Hunter was chief; he went to the north land.

18. Winelowich sakimanep lowushkakiang.

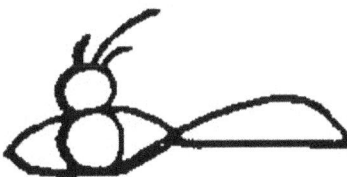

19. Look-About was chief, he went to the Talega mountains.

19. Linkwekinuk sakimanep talegachukang.

PART Vb.

20. East-Villager was chief; he was east of Talega.

20. Wapalawikwan sakimanep waptalegawing.

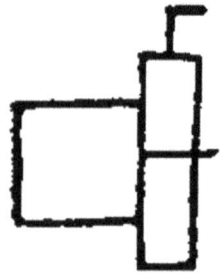

21. A great land and a wide land was the east land,

21. Amangaki amigaki wapakisinep.

22. A land without snakes, a rich land, a pleasant land.

22. Mattakohaki mapawaki mawulitenol.

23. Great Fighter was chief, toward the north.

23. Gikenopalat sakimanep pekochilowan.

24. At the Straight river, River-Loving was chief.

24. Saskwihanang hanaholend sakimanep.

25. Becoming-Fat was chief at Sassafras land.

25. Gattawisi sakimanep winakaking.

26. All the hunters made wampum again at the great sea.

26. Wemi lowichik gishikshawipek lappi kichipek.

27. Red-Arrow was chief at the stream again.

27. Makhiawip sakimanep lapihaneng.

28. The Painted-Man was chief at the Mighty Water.

28. Wolomenap sakimanep maskekitong.

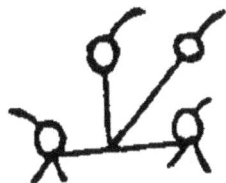

29. The Easterners and the Wolves go northeast.

29. Wapanand tumewand waplowaan.

30. Good-Fighter was chief, and went to the north.

30. Wulitpallat sakimanep piskwilowan.

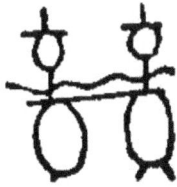

31. The Mengwe, the Lynxes, all trembled.

31. Mahongwi pungelika wemi nungwi.

32. Again an Affable was chief, and made peace with all,

32. Lappi tamenend sakimanepit wemi langundit.

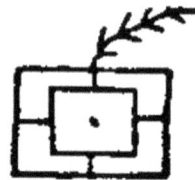

33. All were friends, all were United, under this great chief

33. Wemi nitis wemi takwicken sakima kichwon.

36. Great-Beaver was chief, remaining in Sassafras land.

36. Kichitamak sakimanep winakununda.

37. White-Body was chief on the sea shore.

37. Wapahakey sakimanep sheyabian.

38. Peace-Maker was chief, friendly to all.

38. Elangomel sakimanep makeliwulit.

39. He-Makes-Mistakes was chief, hurriedly coming.

39. Pitenumen sakimanep unchihillen.

PART Vc.

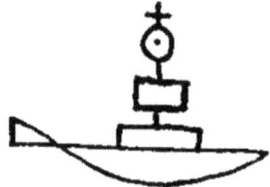

40. At this time whites came on the Eastern sea.

40. Wonwihil wapekunchi wapsipayat.

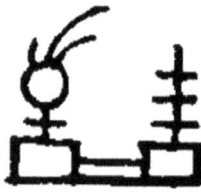

41. Much-Honored was chief; he was prosperous.

41. Makelomush sakimanep wulatenamen.

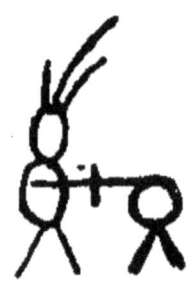

42. Well-Praised was chief; he fought at the south.

42. Wulakeningus sakimanep shawanipalat.

43. He fought in the land of the Talega and Koweta.

43. Otaliwako akowetako ashkipalliton.

44. White-Otter was chief; a friend of the Talamatans.

44. Wapagamoshki sakimanep lamatanitis.

45. White-Horn was chief; he went to the Talega,

45. Wapashum sakimanep talegawunkik.

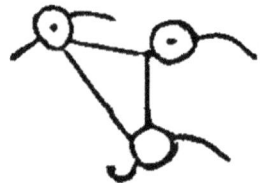

46. To the Hilini, to the Shawnees, to the Kanawhas.

46. Mahiliniki mashawoniki makonowiki.

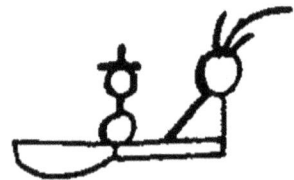

47. Coming-as-a-Friend was chief; he went to the Great Lakes,

47. Nitispayat sakimanep kipemapekan,

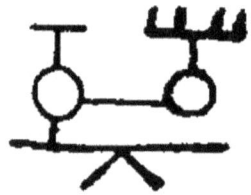

48. Visiting all his children, all his friends.

48. Wemiamik weminitik kiwikhotan.

49. Cranberry-Eater was chief, friend of the Ottawas.

49. Pakimitzin sakimanep tawanitip.

50. North-Walker was chief, he made festivals.

50. Lowaponskan sakimanep ganshowenik.

51. Slow-Gatherer was chief at the shore.

51. Tashawinso sakimanep shayabing.

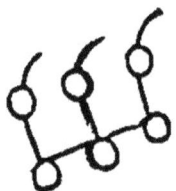

52. As three were desired, three those were who grew forth,

52. Nakhagattamen nakhalissin wenchikit,

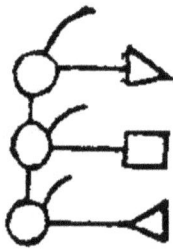

52. bis. The Unami, the Minsi, the Chikini.

52. bis. Unamini minsimini chikimini.

53. Man-Who-Fails was chief; he fought the Mengwe.

53. Epallahchund sakimanep mahongwipallat.

54. He-is-Friendly was chief; he scared the Mengwe.

54. Langomuwi sakimanep mahongwichamen.

55. Saluted was chief; thither,

55. Wangomend sakimanep ikalawit,

56. Over there, on the Scioto, he had foes.

56. Otaliwi wasiotowi shingalusit.

57. White-Crab was chief, a friend of the shore.

57. Wapachikis sakimanep sahyabinitis.

58. Watcher was chief, he looked toward the sea.

58. Nenachihat sakimanep peklinkwekin.

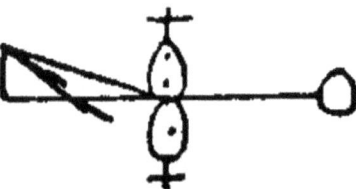

59. At this time, from north and south, the whites came.

59. Wonwihil lowashawa wapayachik.

60. They are peaceful; they have great things; who are they?

60. Langomuwak kitohatewa ewenikiktit?

www.ingramcontent.com/pod-product-compliance
Lightning Source LLC
Chambersburg PA
CBHW051553010526
44118CB00022B/2684